Master the Art of Unreal Engine 4 - Blueprints

Extra Credits - Saving & Loading + Unreal Motion Graphics!

Master the Art of Unreal Engine 4 - Blueprints - Extra Credits (Saving & Loading + Unreal Motion Graphics!)

First Published: 28/09/2014
Production Reference: 014180SOLID14045

ISBN-13: 978-1500313784
ISBN-10: 1500313785

www.kitatusstudios.co.uk
Cover image by Ryan Shah (contact@kitatusstudios.co.uk)

Credits

Author

Ryan Shah

Special Thanks

Scarlett Juzzle

- Thank-You Scarlett for putting up with me over all this time and believing in every crazy idea that comes into my head! I've had such an amazing time being with you and I can't wait for every step of our future. I hope you look forward to even more of my crazy ideas!

Epic Games

- Thank-you for being awesome!

About the Author

Ryan Shah is Project Lead / Lead Developer at Kitatus Studios. Boasting over 10 years of experience creating video-games, Ryan has worked on an assortment of different programs to create video-game experiences.

Before Kitatus Studios, Ryan was a freelance writer, who self-published works of fiction. Using his experience as a writer, Ryan turned to video-games, a life-long passion to bring the worlds of his ideas to life.

He can be found online at http://kitatusstudios.co.uk and can be contacted at contact@kitatusstudios.co.uk

Acknowledgement

A huge thank-you and a half has to go to my beautiful girlfriend Scarlett, who no matter what has always believed in me when nobody else did. Her patience is inspiring.

I'd like Epic for creating such a diverse yet easy to use system with Unreal Engine 4. When people say it's a game changer, they weren't wrong!

I'd also like to thank you, the reader. I might not know you personally, but by you buying this book - You're helping to support me and helping to support the video-game industry. Who knows - Maybe this book will help you and become the stepping stone you need to make the BEST GAME OF ALL TIME. Anything is possible!

Table of Contents

Preface

Unreal Engine 4 is the latest version of the popular video-game development package; the Unreal Engine. The Unreal Engine needs no introduction; Being the powerhouse behind the previous console generation from the start. To call the Unreal Engine a powerhouse would be an understatement, the Unreal Engine is everything a developer (Indie and Commercial) would ever need in a video-game engine to create their ideal project. With it's latest iteration, Unreal Engine 4, Epic has improved Unreal Engine and propelled the engine into the next-generation, they have brought the future to the present with Unreal Engine 4 and there's literally never been a better time to begin using Unreal Engine 4 for any project, big or small, commercial or independent.

Mastering the Art of Unreal Engine 4 - Blueprints (Extra Credits) takes a concise, clear, informative but fun approach to developing Unreal Engine 4, without touching a single line of code. By using this book, you'll be creating various small projects completely in blueprint. From this book, you'll be equipped with the know-how you'll need to create the game of your dreams. On top of mastering the Blueprints system in Unreal Engine 4, you'll also learn the secrets behind getting the most out of the beast of an engine.

What You'll Need For This Book

In order to take full advantage of this book; You'll need a Windows, Mac or Linux computer that is capable of running Unreal Engine 4. It requires a computer with the following system configuration, which doubles up at the "Minimum Requirements" for this book:

- Desktop PC or Mac
- Windows 7 64-bit or Mac OS X 10.9.2 or later
- Quad-core Intel or AMD processor, 2.5 GHz or faster
- NVIDIA GeForce 470 GTX or AMD Radeon 6870 HD series card or higher
- 8 GB RAM

Note: Believe it or not, You'll also need Unreal Engine 4 (Version 4.4 or newer).

Who this Book is For

Mastering the Art of Unreal Engine 4 - Blueprints (Extra Credits) is designed for anyone whose dreamt of creating video-games, but didn't have the knowhow to. This book is also designed for everyone who want to harness the power of Unreal Engine 4 to take their creations to the next level and beyond and the people who want to create games without writing a single line of code.

Those who are familiar with Unreal Engine 4 will have an easier time, but everything in the book is explained clearly and with reference screenshots to make the process of mastering the blueprints system in Unreal Engine 4 a breeze. People with no prior experience to using Unreal Engine 4, or game engines in general should have no problem with following this book, but if you need additional help with anything in the book, feel free to ask on the Unreal Engine Forums (http://forums.unrealengine.com) or email me directly: contact@kitatusstudios.co.uk.

Reader Feedback

I love feedback! Good or bad, it's all welcome and I highly recommend you do so! If you loved reading or hated it, I seriously would love to know. Feedback is important in helping letting me know how I've done, what needs to be fixed and I'm just generally intrigued on how well / bad I've done. I'm a perfectionist and I strive for the best, so if there's anything I can improve on, feel free to email: contact@kitatusstudios.co.uk

Customer Support

Since you're the owner of this book, You have the opportunity to get bonus content, such as colour images and project content: Head to http://content.Kitatusstudios.co.uk to access to these files!

Piracy

I'm not going to pretend it doesn't exist; Piracy is piracy and nothing is going to stop it. If you've pirated this book; It's alright. I'm not going to curse you or anything. It's sad that you're not willing to spend money on this book, but I know times are tough and in the digital world I know that everything is free to some people.

Due to the fact I've given up the time to write this book to help teach others to harness the power of Blueprints, losing out on work hours and time I could have spent on **Super Distro** (My first Commercially to-be-released project), I ask that if you pirated this book and you've enjoyed this book, Please consider purchasing Super Distro or you could send a donation through my website. This means that even if you don't spend the full-price on this book, My efforts to bring these tutorials to you aren't 100% in vein.

If you've purchased this book, then I can't thank-you enough for supporting me and my work and I seriously am grateful you're experiencing the book through legitimate means.

Errata

At the time of writing, the book has no errors. However, as the engine is updated, things might change. In the unlikely event some of the code no longer works, please email me immediately: contact@kitatusstudios.co.uk - By doing this, you not only secure the integrity of the book, but you also help others by not coming across errors and this leads to a stress-free experience with this book. Who knows, you might also be credited in later book revisions!

Downloading DLC (Downloadable Content)

You can download colour variations of the images in this book, as well as UE4 project files from http://content.kitatusstudios.co.uk.

Questions

If you have any questions, email me at contact@kitatusstudios.co.uk. The line is open, so please don't be afraid to get in touch.

Mission #1 - Title Screen

Creating a Title Screen and Options Menu!

Template:
> Third-Person Blueprint

What You'll Learn:
> - How to use Unreal Motion Graphics
> - How to set options in Unreal Engine 4

What You'll Need:
> - Background Texture (For Title Screen) [1280 x 720 or 1920 x 1080]

[Extras] What You'll Need:
> - Animated Material (At least 720p would work perfectly)

Let's Begin!

Hello again one and all and welcome to the next installment of Master the Art of Unreal Engine 4 - Blueprints; Where we will be covering lots of little goodies to help boost your Unreal Engine 4 knowledge.

Today we're tackling a title screen, using the (At the time of writing) still experimental tool: "Unreal Motion Graphics". This tool is (Again, at time of writing) still in it's infancy but it's power is leaking out of the sides (Not literally, of course!) - You can do so many things with Unreal Motion Graphics (Such as HUD, Menus and so much more!) - Once you've read through this mini-tutorial, you could even go back to Book #1 and compare UMG to the classic way of creating a HUD!

I'm so stoked to be showing you the ropes of UMG so I am just going to dive straight into things! Are you ready to learn even more Awesome stuff?! Hensin A-Go Go!

Step #1 - Create a new Unreal Engine project (Make sure it's on at least Unreal Engine 4.4.1, anything earlier then version doesn't have Unreal Motion Graphics!)

[NOTE: It really doesn't matter what project you use as a template, but I recommend the "Third-Person Blueprint" template as that is what I'll be using for this!]

Now you should have something similar to this screen:

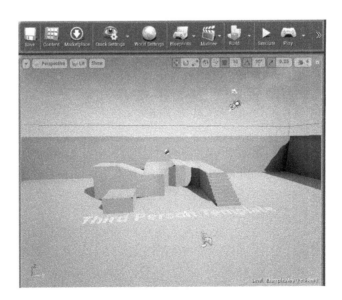

Doesn't that feel like home now? It never gets old seeing this screen!

Before we carry on, if you're living in the present time (And not in the distant future!), you'll need to activate Unreal Motion Graphics (As it's currently an experimental feature!). To do that:

Step #2 - Go to Edit (In the top-left of your Unreal Engine window, next to File) and select "Editor Preferences".

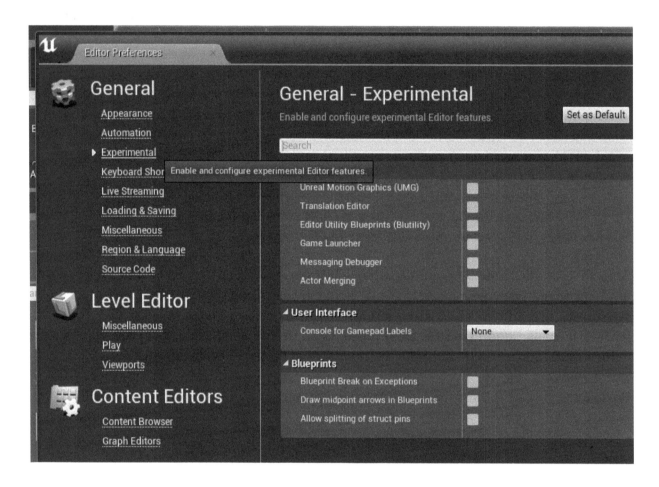

Step #3 - In the "Editor Preferences" window, click "Experimental" which is under the General header, which will open up the Experimental section.

From here, you can see "Unreal Motion Graphics (UMG)" on the right. Currently it's unticked. All you have to do is click the empty box to activate it (Make sure the box is filled in to signify it has been activated!)

Step #4 - Once you have activated "Unreal Motion Graphics (UMG)", make sure to click the "Set as Default" button on the top of the "Editor Preferences" window, then you can close the window and go back to the main engine screen.

Before we continue, there's two more quick things we need to do:

Step #5 - Save your project as it is (Just to be safe!)

Step #6 - Close Unreal Engine 4 (Your Project and the Launcher), wait a few seconds and re-open Unreal Engine 4 (And then your project!)

NOTE: Remember to open your project in Engine version 4!

EXTRA NOTE: Don't play this one cool. I know when you install programs, some of you hit the "Restart later" button and continue to use the program like a rebel, but don't do that here because that doesn't work. You HAVE to restart the editor or Unreal Motion Graphics won't work properly!

Step #7 - Now that you've restarted your project, we need to create a new empty level. Call this new level "UMG_MainMenu" and make sure you select "Empty Level".

Save the level as it currently is and then we can begin the fun stuff!

Creating a UMG Blueprint!

Step #1 - Within the Content Browser, (Making sure you've got the "GAME" folder highlighted) create a new folder (By clicking New > Folder). Name this folder "UMG".

Step #2 - Once the folder has been created, double click "UMG" to open up the folder.

Now we're going to have some fun!

Step #3 - While still in the Content Browser (In our "UMG" folder), Right Click (Ctrl + Click) in the empty space in the folder (Which brings up the "Create" window). In this window, Scroll down to User Interface and highlight "User Interface" with your mouse, when the pop-up menu opens, select "Widget Blueprint" (Name this Blueprint "UMG_MiniTitle")

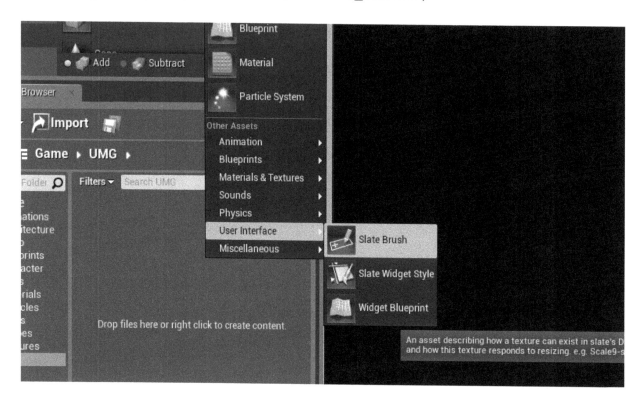

Step #4 - Double-Click the newly created "UMG_MiniTitle" to open up Unreal Motion Graphics; Now then fun REALLY begins!

Creating our Title Screen!

First things first, we're greeted with a "CanvasPanel" already placed down for us (You can see this in the bottom left under "Hierarchy". We don't need a CanvasPanel for what we're going to do, so...

Step #1 - Click on the "CanvasPanel" entry in the hierarchy and press delete on your Keyboard to do away with the useless "CanvasPanel".

Now we've got rid of the CanvasPanel, we can put in a border, which will cover our game screen edge-to-edge which will be perfect for our Main Menu background!

To create a border, we have to first find where it is hidden in UMG (Which is actually not that hidden, I mean if it were Solid Snake, it would be dead in seconds!)

Step #2 - In the "Palette" (In the top-left of the UMG window), there are a number of options just waiting to be clicked on.

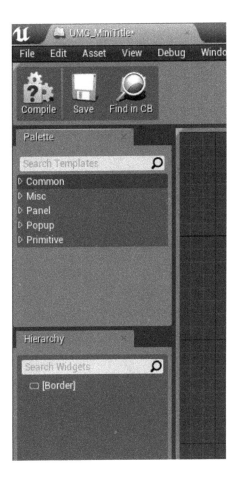

If you click on "Common", a whole new range of options are now at our disposal. To put the border into our project, all we have to do is click "Border" and drag it into the Blueprint-looking UMG view. You'll know if you've done it right as it'll now show up in the Hierarchy!

To some this wouldn't seem like doing much, but if you compare this to the HUD we created last time round, we technically created a HUD blueprint, set the resolution of the screen that the user is using and got it primed to create our HUD... In literally seconds!

Step #3 - Now our Border is ready, we can fill it with an image. To do this, we need to create a "Slate Brush". It sounds complicated but it takes a good couple of seconds.

Close out of UMG for a second and go back to the Content Browser, into your UMG folder. This is the time to import your image for the background if you haven't already (1280 x 720 image or 1920 x 1080 is ideal!)

Step #4 - Once your image has been imported, we can now create our brush. Just like you created the Widget Blueprint, do the same thing but choose Slate Widget (If you've forgotten, Right Click [Ctrl + Click] > User Interface > Slate Widget) and name this UI_Title.

Your folder should now look something like this:

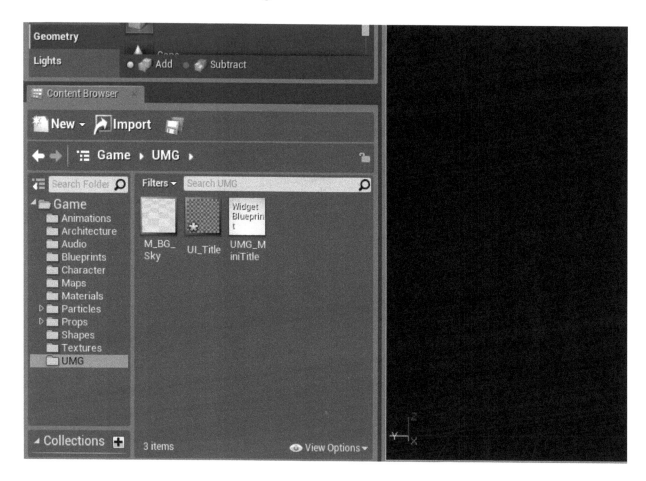

NOTE: I've already created a Material for my texture but it's down to you whether or not you want to do that.

EXTRA NOTE: Now is a good time to save!

Step #5 - Double click "UI_Title" to open up the properties, and set your "Texture or Material Asset" to your image that you have imported!

Before you move on, make sure you set the image size correctly or this will cause issues!

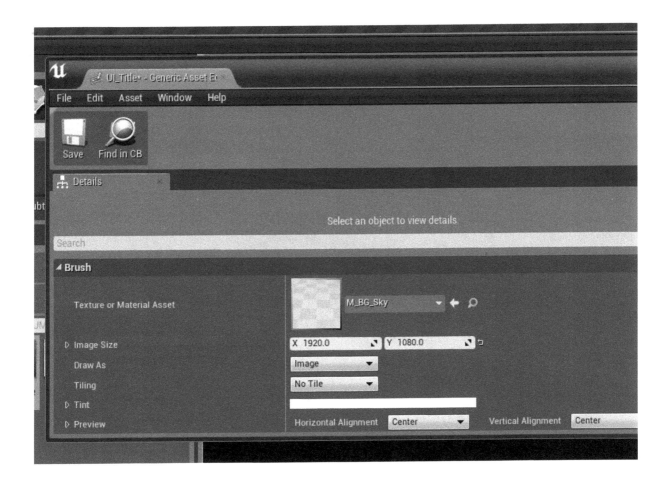

NOTE: If you're importing a Material, it might say that "This Material is not supported in UI". If this is the case, simply double click your material from within the content browser and in the properties (On the left in the Material Editor), scroll down till you see "Used with UI" and set that to true, compile, save and then all your problems that UMG is churning out should disappear!

Once you're happy with everything, save and close this window and head back into "UMG_MiniTitle"

Step #6 - Once back in UMG, Go into the Hierarchy and click "Border". This will bring up the properties on the right-hand side.

Just under "Appearance", where it says "Brush" and has a big empty white box, Simply click "None" and swap it with your Slate Brush.

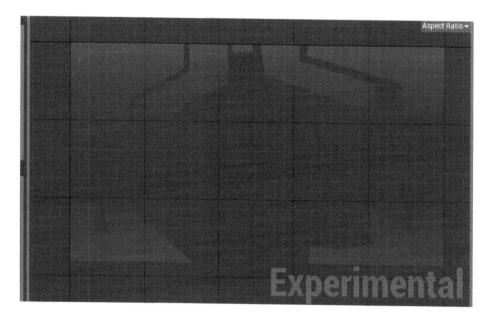

Done! Now our background image is showing, let's get making our title screen!

Buttons, Buttons, Buttons!

Now we have a background image, we need to put a button into our Title Screen so the user can navigate around, play the game, change their settings or exit your project.

To create buttons, we need to create a box that can sit on our Title Screen. To do this...

Step #1 - Head back to the Palette on the top-left and this time instead of using tools from the "Common" section, click "Panel" to bring up tools that will be extremely helpful to our cause!

This is where we need to bring the Canvas Panel back, so...

Step #2 - Simply click "Canvas Panel" and drag it into the viewport of UMG. Done.

Just to be safe, check the Hierarchy quickly to make sure the "CanvasPanel" is now sitting under the "Border" like so:

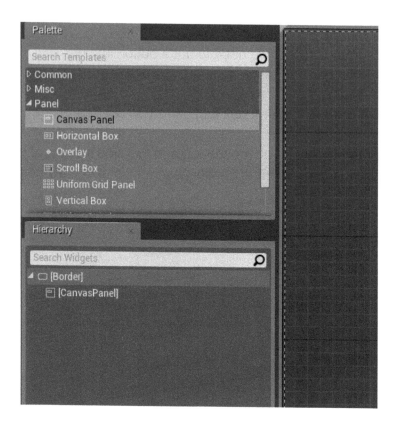

Now we can start adding buttons and whatnot to our Widget!

Step #3 - In the Hierarchy, click "CanvasPanel" to make sure what we add next goes into the CanvasPanel and not on the Border.

Once you've highlighted the CanvasPanel in the Hierachy, go back to the "Palette" box and this time click "Horizontal Box" and drag into our UMG viewport.

Step #4 - Zoom in (By using your mouse's Scroll Wheel) to the Horizontal Box and click the newly created Horizontal Box and re-size the box to cover where a long button would sit. Once you've re-sized the box, move the box near the bottom of the screen like so by clicking and dragging the box:

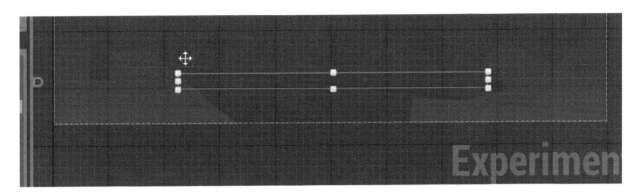

We've now created the "House" for the button, so what's next? Just before we put our button in his house to sleep, we need to tell UMG one important thing...

We need to tell UMG that no matter what the screen size, our button needs to stay in this position at the bottom of the screen. And this is how we do just that!

Step #5 - With the "Horizontal Box" still selected, go to it's options on the right of the screen and at the top under "Layout" is a section called "Anchors", it looks like this:

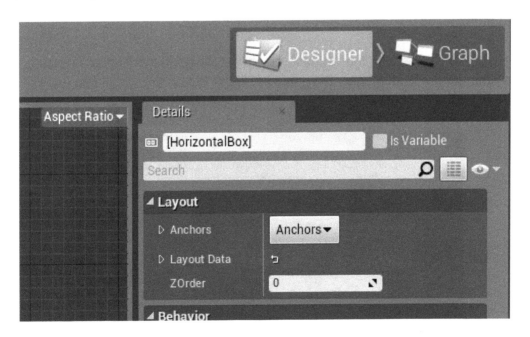

Step #6 - Under "Anchors" there is a grey box with the word "Anchors" written inside with a down arrow, click this down arrow and select the 10th option (Small box in the bottom centre).

This stops the button disappearing no matter what the size of the screen!

So we have the "House" all set up, it's time to put the button in it's home!

Step #7 - Head back to the "Palette" box in the left and go to the "Common" section. Within this common section, click Button and drag it INTO your Horizontal Box which you set up previously.

There's still some work left to be done before this is a fully functioning button!

The button is looking a little bare at the moment, so let's get some text inside so players find out what our button should do!

Step #8 - Just like you did with the "Button", find "Text Block" in the Palette (Which is under "Common" just like the Button was). Drag this INTO the button and you'll see just like magic the text becomes part of our button.

Step #9 - With the text selected, just like before head over to the "Details" panel on the right. This time, we need to edit the text… So just under "Content", there's a section called "Text". So can you guess what we have to do with this…? You got it!

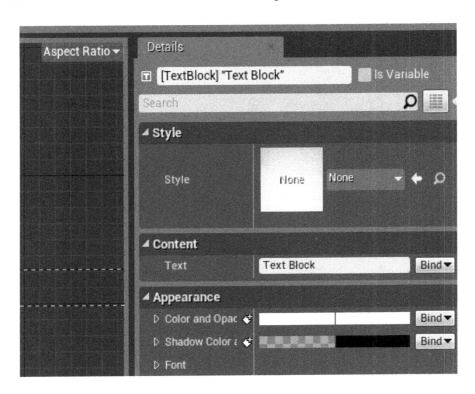

In the text box, write: "Click to Start".

I bet you're itching to know what the "Bind" button is for; But **DO NOT CLICK IT**… Just yet. We'll come back to this soon!

There's just one little thing and we're done with this button for the time being:

Step #10 - Click the "Button" (Not the text) and go into the "Details" on the right. Scroll down until you find the "Layout" section. In this section, there's a part called "Padding" and just under that is a part called "Size" with two options: "Auto" and "Fill".

Click Auto to make it fill our Horizontal Box.

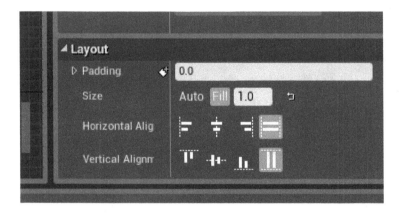

We've done what needed to be done now for this button; But it's not quite functional just yet.

Before we continue however, we need to create another Widget Blueprint, so for now:

Step #11 - "Compile" / Save and close this UMG window and in our UMG folder Right Click (Ctrl + Click) our "UMG_MiniTitle" and select "Create Copy".

Name this copy: "UMG_Title2".

Main Menu D-I-Y!

Now it's time to test your skills so I can show to you just how much you've learnt without realising it!

Your UMG folder should now look like this:

If it does, Awesome! We can continue; If not, however, then simply double-back and skim over the last chapter to check if you've missed something.

Ready to continue? Excellent!

Step #1 - Double-Click "UMG_Title2" to open up our duplicated Menu.

Step #2 - Expand all of the objects in the Hierarchy and delete the Horizontal Box, Button and Text (Deleting the Horizontal Box should delete it all for you!)

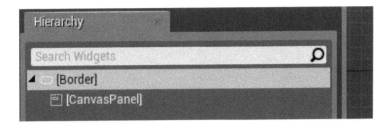

Step #3 - Now use what you've learnt so far to create this:

Remember to anchor everything to the CENTRE of the screen this time (Not the bottom) and make sure each of the buttons are in their own Horizontal Box but they're all a "Child" of the CanvasPanel.

If you need help, refresh yourself by going through the past chapter, but I believe in you and I know you can do it with no problems whatsoever!

Link to the Past

So we have a Title Screen and a Main Menu, but nothing hooking them both together. I bet you're raring to know just how to link them together; So what we are waiting for? Let's do it!

Step #1 - Save / Compile your "UMG_Title2". Once saved, close "UMG_Title2" and open "UMG_MiniTitle".

Step #2 - Click on our "Click to Start" button (Be sure to not click the text!) and head over to the details panel on the right:

Where it says "Events", there's a section called "On Clicked Event" with a "Bind" button. This means we can tell UMG what will happen when this button has been pressed, so click Bind and select "Create Binding". This will create a Blueprint for us, ready for us to mess around with.

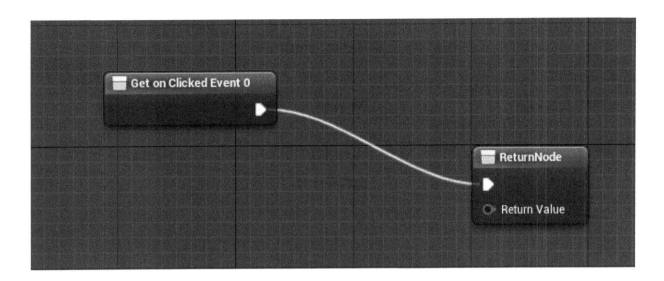

First things first, we need to break this connection as at the moment the Blueprint reads: "Start the stuff in this line > End the stuff in this line". This, obviously isn't what we want.

Step #3 - Alt+Click the arrow on the Get on Clicked Event 0 to break the connection. Now click the "Get on Click Event" node and move it a bit further to left so we have some room to play with.

Step #4 - From the empty pin on the right of "Get on Clicked Event", click and drag to the right and our favourite "Compact Blueprint Library" will open up.

Type in "Remove" and select "Remove from Viewport", this will take our current title and get rid of it.

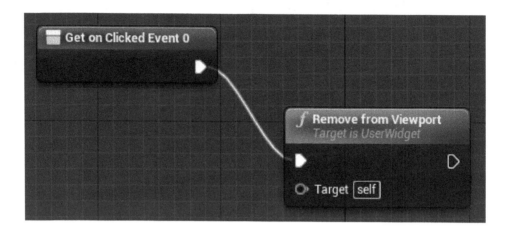

Now that we've gotten rid of the current Title Screen, we need to create the other Title Screen we created ("UMG_Title2") so it acts as a seamless transition from Title to Main Menu.

Step #5 - From the empty pin on the right of the "Remove from Viewport" node, click and drag to the right. When the CBL opens up, type in "Create Widget" and select the Create Widget node to create it.

Step #6 - Within the "Create Widget" node, there is a section called "Widget Type", with a box called "Select Class". Click "Select Class" and click "UMG_Title2_C".

This creates the second title screen, but it doesn't actually show our Title screen, it only creates it. It sounds a bit complicated, but all should make sense in a moment.

Step #7 - From the "Return Value" pin of "Create Widget", Click the blue pin and drag to the right. In the Blueprint Library, type "Add" and select "Add to Viewport".

This will bring the second title screen up, but there's a number of bools we need to tick in this node before we can use it as a Title Screen:

Modal & Show Cursor - Set these to true

Modal means the Title Screen eats up all of the inputs, so you don't accidently click behind the title screen.

Show Cursor shows the cursor.

Don't set Absolute to true as when Absolute is false means that it should take up the whole screen and not only part of it.

Step #8 - Now connect the empty right-hand side pin of "Add to Viewport" to the "Return Node" that was originally in this Blueprint and pow! That's this Blueprint done! Save and Compile the Blueprint then close UMG; It's time to tell our project to actually display these menu screens!

Let's See Our Menus!

Head into your empty level and like we've done a few times in the previous book, head into the level blueprint. If you've forgotten how to do this:

> #1 - Click the "Blueprints" button above the viewport
> #2 - Press "Open Level Blueprint

Now the Level Blueprint is open; We need to tell the Level that when the level begins, draw our menu!

As we have the first menu that draws the second menu on the button press, all we have to tell the level blueprint is to draw the first menu. So what are we waiting for?!

Step #1 - Right Click (Ctrl + Click) in empty space in the Blueprint area. When the "Compact Blueprint Library" opens up, type in "Begin" and select "Event Begin Play".

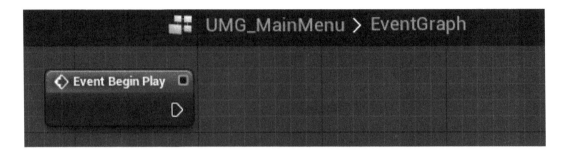

Just like before in the previous chapter, create a "Create Widget" node connected to "Event Begin Play" and then create an "Add to Viewport" node connected to the "Create Widget" node by dragging from the "Return Value" pin.

Once you've created the "Add to Viewport" node, be sure to enable the "Modal" and "Show Cursor" bools again by ticking them!

The only thing you should be doing different from before (Apart from obviously missing out the "Remove from Viewport" node!) is setting the "Widget Type" in the "Create Widget Node" to "UMG_MiniTitle_C".

NOTE: If your UMG files aren't showing up in "Widget Type" this means that one of your Widgets have had issues compiling; Usually because you forgot to connect the "Return Node" in the buttons together!

Once your level blueprint has been updated with: Event Begin Play > Create Widget > Add to Viewport as explained above, Compile the Blueprint, close the Blueprint editor and test your current project by pressing: Alt + P on your keyboard.

Congratulations! It works!

We still need to code the "New Game", "Options" and "Quit Game" buttons (Let's not get ahead of ourselves just yet! There's still one or two obstacles in our way but we'll get there in no-time!)

But this causes for a celebration; You've just created a fully working Title-Screen; So let's get the other buttons working!

Extra Buttons!

Once you've tested your menu and you're completely happy with everything; It's time to program the buttons in our "UMG_Title2" UMG Widget!

Step #1 - In the Content Browser, Open up "UMG_Title2".

Step #2 - Just like in the chapter before the chapter just gone; Create a "Bind" for all three buttons ("New Game", "Options" and "Quit Game") but don't fill out the Blueprints yet.

Once you've created "Binds" for all three buttons, go into the "Graph" tab (On the top-right) and make sure your "Functions" (In the "Variable Library" on the left) look like this:

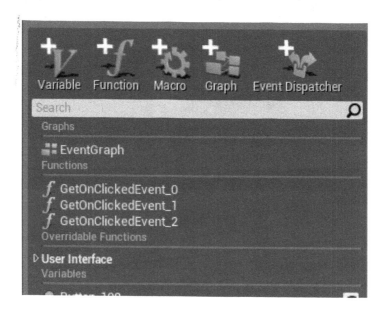

If your "Functions" doesn't look like that, then you haven't created Binds for all three buttons; Go back until you end up with "GetOnClickEvent_0", "GetOnClickEvent_1" and "GetOnClickEvent_2" in the "Functions" area of your UMG Blueprint.

Ready to continue? Awesome!

Open up the Blueprint for "GetOnClickEvent_0" (Which should be bound to the "New Game" button).

All we have to do for this is hook up a "Open Level" node!

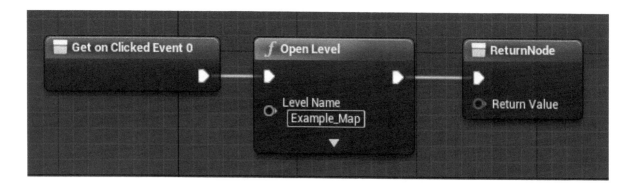

Within the "Open Level" node, there is an input called "Level Name". For demonstration purposes, let's put in "Example_Map", which will open the Example Map within our project!

What did we just do? - Basically the Blueprint reads: When the Button is clicked, open "Example_Map"! Simple... yet effective!

Compile and move over to the Blueprint "GetOnClickedEvent2" [Which should be bound to your "Quit Game" button].

I'm not talking about the "Options Button" (Which is "GetOnClickedEvent1". Do not open "GetOnClickedEvent1", open "GetOnClickedEvent2").

When you're in your "Quit Game" Blueprint ("GetOnClickedEvent2"), we need to add a "Execute Console Command" node, which is a node which (You guessed it!) executes a console command!

By now, I'm sure you can guess how to create the node, but if not, here's a hint: Right Click (Ctrl + Click). When the Compact Blueprint Library opens up, type in "Execute Console" and select the correct node!

Now, I'm sure you're wondering what "Command" needs to go into the input within "Execute Console Command", so let's not waste any time!

Within the "Command" input, simply type "Quit". Yup, that's all you have to do for this Blueprint!

So just like that, we've set up "New Game" and the "Quit Game", we're almost all done with this project! All we have to do now is couple up everything we've learnt so far as well as a few more pointers to create the "Options" menu!

These Are Your Options!

Create a new Widget Blueprint and call it "UMG_Options". Within this menu, use everything you've learned thus far to create three buttons (All with text in!), some text above these buttons and two more buttons underneath the other buttons and text. You should get something that looks like this:

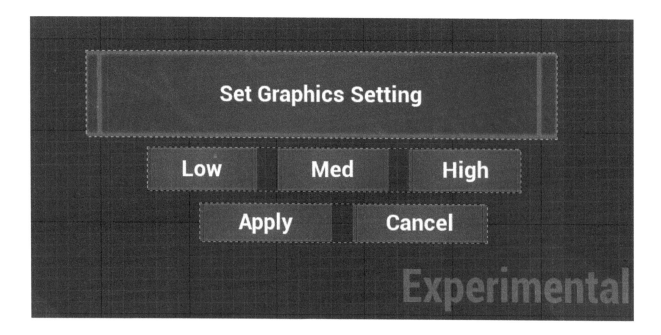

If you can't see the image, here's what you need in the relative boxes and whatnot:

- Top text box: "Set Graphics Settings"
- Three buttons under the Text Box: "Low, Med, High"
- The two buttons under the "Low, Med, High" - "Apply" and "Cancel"

Got it? Awesome! If not, Skim back through what we've already covered in the book to touch up on whatever you're missing.

Once you're ready to continue, we need to head over into the Event Graph of our "UMG_Options" (Remember to use the top ribbon to navigate!).

Just like we learnt in the last book, we need to create an Integer. Remember that? If not, here's a real quick reminder of what an Integer is and how to create one:

What is an Integer? - An Integer is a number that we can set and call back to later. Why is this important? Because we can change things if our Integer is a specific number!

"But Ryan, Why can't I use a Float? Isn't that a number we can set too?" -Well, Mystical reader who can write and be answered ala Harry Potter to Tom Riddle; A Float can deal with decimal places, which is great for storing time or anything that needs a number.number figure, but an Integer doesn't deal with decimals, It just doesn't understand them.

Instead, it prides itself on acting as a switch or a collection for WHOLE numbers only (Sorry decimal numbers, it's to the Float for you!)

"Sounds cool! But why do we need that right now?" Well, Mr / Miss / Ms / Dr, we can use an Integer to switch between Low, Med and High with almost no effort at all! We can then save that Integer and call it back WHENEVER we need it again!

"Groovitational! Let's Make One!" - Sure thing! Let's get right to it!

[NOTE: Yes, it was 5am when I wrote that, Don't mind me!]

Step #1 - If you're not there already, head into the "Graph" tab of your "UMG_Options". (Use the top-right Tab to navigate to it!)

Step #2 - On the far left, there's a window that I like to call the "Variable Library", it looks a little like this:

Step #3 - Click the "Variable" button (Which is next to Function, Macro .etc), to create a new Variable.

Step #4 - Within the details panel (Just below the "Variable Library"!), change the "Variable Type" to Int and set the name to "GraphicsSettings".

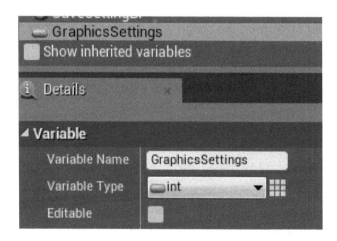

Step #5 - Done? Awesome! That's all we need to do here for the moment, so use the top-right ribbon again and go back into the "Designer" tab to go back to our UMG!

Step #6 - Click the "Low" button which you created earlier (Not the text, the button!) and in the right-hand side details panel, create a new Bind for it (Just like we did before!)

Step #7 - This will open a Blueprint editor for what happens when this button is pressed. On the left in your "Variable Library", grab your "GraphicsSettings" (You might need to scroll down in the "Variable Library" to find it!) and drag it into the Blueprint area. When asked, select "Set".

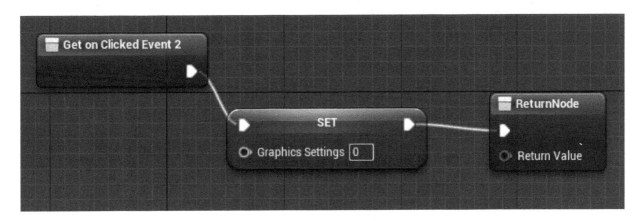

Step #8 - As this button will be the "Low" setting, keep the "GraphicsSetting" at 0 and connect both left and right white inputs to the "GetOnClickedEvent" and "ReturnNode" respectively.

Step #9 - Do exactly what we just did for both the "Med" and "High" buttons, however remember to set "GraphicsSettings" to 1 in the Mid Blueprint and 2 in the High Blueprint. Confused? Here's what you should end up with:

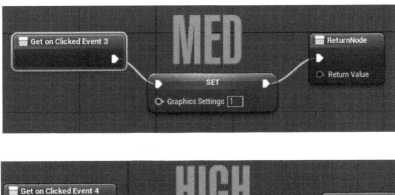

Step #10 - Three buttons down, two to go! We'll deal with Apply in two moments, but first let's take on that "Cancel" button. Create a binding for it and just like what we did from the "Title Screen" to "Options", create a "Remove for Viewport" node followed by "Create Widget" (Remember to select "UMG_Title2" in "Widget Type"!) followed by "Add to Viewport":

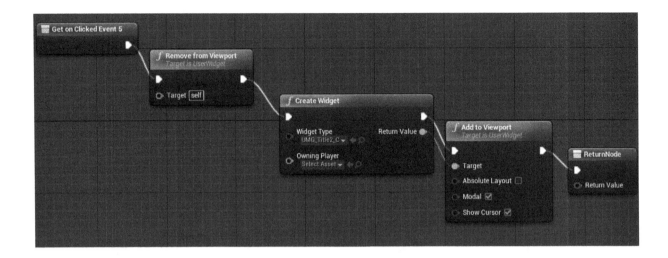

Step #11 - We've now only got one Button left to fill in; "Apply!". So what are we waiting for? Create a bind for "Apply" and let's get to coding!

Step #12 - Right Click (Ctrl+Click) to open the "Compact Blueprint Library" and type in "Switch on Int".

Step #13 - Click the "Switch On It" Node which we just created and in the "Details" panel underneath the "Variable Library", set "Default Pin" to false by unchecking the box. Once done, within the "Switch on Int" node, add two more "Pins".

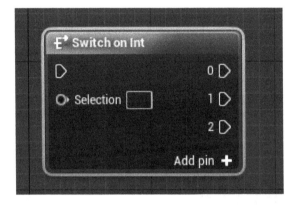

Step #14 - Doesn't that light green button next to "Selection" seem familiar? You've guessed it! Grab your "GraphicsSettings" from the "Variable Library", drag it into the Blueprint and select "Get" when asked. Hook it into Selection and connect the left input pin of the "Switch on Int" into the "GetOnClickedEvent"

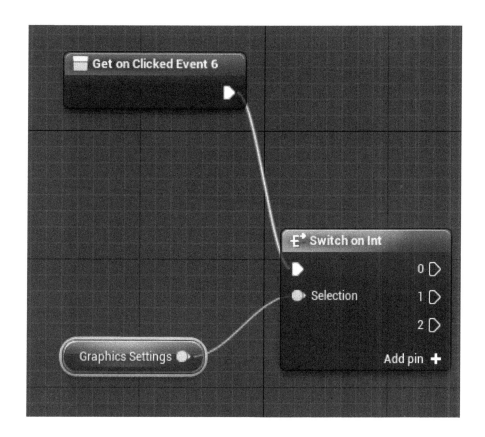

Notice that we've created three "Switch On Int" outputs: 0, 1 and 2. Just like we did with "GraphicsSettings" Integer. So can you guess what this means? You got it! 0 Stands for our "Low" option, "Med" for our Medium and "High" for our High option. But how do we change the graphics quality? Simple!

Step #15 - Right Click (Ctrl + Click) to open up the "Compact Blueprint Library" and type in "Execute Console" and select "Execute Console Command". Do this three times.

Step #16 - Hook each one of these nodes into the outputs of "Switch on Int", like so:

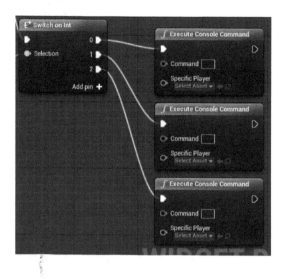

Now we need to figure out what Command to use; A quick check of the "Engine Scalability" page on the Unreal Engine site gives us a number of options to play with. For this tutorial's sake, we'll just be using "sg.PostProcessQuality".

For low, we'll use "sg.PostProcessQuality 0", Medium we'll use: "sg.PostProcessQuality 1" and for High: "sg.PostProcessQuality 3".

Step #17 - So in the "Command" area of our "Execute Console Command", in the one that stems from "Switch on Int 0" put "sg.PostProcessQuality 0". In the one stemming from "1", put "sg.PostProcessQuality 1" and "sg.PostProcessQuality 3" respectively.

So what now? I bet you're thinking we've got to do some super-complicated stuff? Nope! Simply do what we've done a few times now - Create a "Remove for Viewport" node followed by "Create Widget" (Remember to select "UMG_Title2" in "Widget Type"!) followed by "Add to Viewport".

Connect all three "Console Command" outputs to the input of "Remove from Viewport" and connect the output of "Add to Viewport" to the main output of our Blueprint like so and we're done!

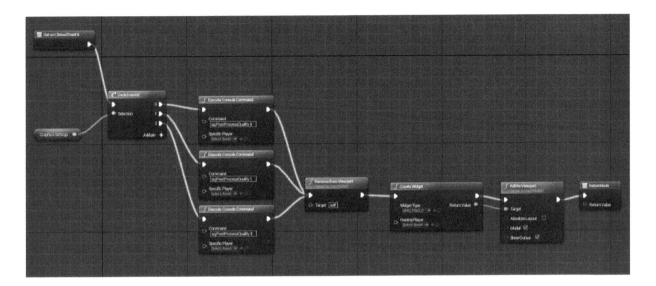

Now it's finished! We can tap ourselves on the shoulder now; We've created a working menu system! But wait... What good is this menu system if it doesn't save our preferences?

Oh-ho-ho-ho, It seems impossible but it's far more simpler then you think. But we'll save that for the next Mini-Mission! So what are you waiting for?! You made an awesome menu, now let's make it 110% more awesome!

Mission #2 - Saving & Loading

Auto-Saving & Loading our Settings!

Template:
Third-Person Blueprint

What You'll Learn:
- Saving & Loading

What You'll Need:
- The Options Menu You Created In The Last Chapter or Use The ArtOfBP_Mini#1
Project available at http://content.kitatusstudios.co.uk

Henshin A-Go-Go Baby!

Let's not dilly-dally, let's get right back into things!

Step #1 - If you're not there already, open up the Menu project we created in the last chapter; Or if you don't have that to hand, download and open the "ArtOfBP_Mini1" project files available at: http://content.kitatusstudios.co.uk

We need to create a SaveGame blueprint to store our Settings in which we've created, so head into the "UMG" folder within the Content Browser" and go to "New > Blueprint".

When it asks what type of Blueprint you'd like to create, click the "Custom Classes" button near the bottom of the Window and in the search field, type "Save" and select "SaveGame":

Step #2 - Click "Select" and name this Blueprint: "Save_SaveGraphics". Once created, double click the newly-created Blueprint to open it up. There's not a terrible amount we have to do in here; But it's crucial you don't get it wrong or none of the awesome we're about to achieve will actually work!

Step #3 - Once your Blueprint has loaded up, head over to the "Variable Library" (In the Graph tab!) and create a new Int (You remember how to, right? If not, go and skim the last chapter again!) and call it "S_Graphics".

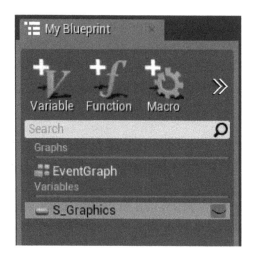

Save & Compile this Blueprint then you can close it!

That's all we have to do for the Save blueprint!

"What?! But how does that work?!" I hear your mind scream through these pages.

Well, it's a little more complicated then what you're assuming. This Save Blueprint doesn't actually save or even load information. The Blueprint stores information that can be called at anytime. Think of it as a pocket.

A pocket doesn't have hands, so it can't give you the chocolate bar you've put in there and it can't add more chocolate bars to itself (Imagine that...) but what it does is store that Chocolate until you need it next.

So what do we have to do now? We need to create those virtual hands to feed our pocket with Chocolate bars!

Before we continue, I'd like to mention why we're about to do things the way we're about to do things - I've tried many combinations of castings and whatnot but a lot of the casting cases don't seem to work with the current Unreal Motion Graphics version in the current Unreal Engine 4 build. The way we're about to follow seems to work at the moment however!

In the main view of your Unreal Engine window (The one with the "Game View!"), There's a ribbon at the top, just above the in-game view (We covered this in Book #1!). You have a number of options in the top ribbon, such as "Quick Settings, World Settings, Blueprints, Matinee" .etc)

Step #4 - Click "World Settings", which will option a details panel in the right (Where "Details" usually are).

Step #5 - Scroll down to "GameMode" in the World Settings window, and press the "New" button. Name this GameMode Blueprint "MainMenuGameMode".

If you can't see the "Selected GameMode" options, click the Grey right arrow next to "Selected GameMode" to expand the window.

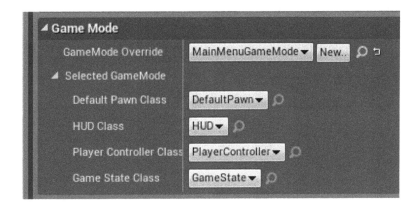

We need to create a "Player Controller", which will act as the conduit between our UMG and Save Blueprint.

Head back to our "UMG" folder and create a new Blueprint. When the "Pick Parent Class" window opens up, select Player Controller.

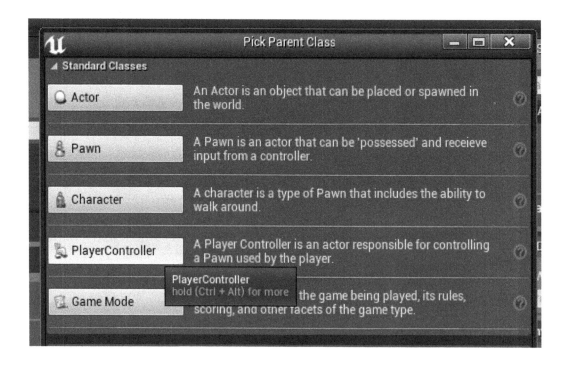

Name this Blueprint "PC_MainMenu". Now head back to the "World Settings" GameMode area and set the PlayerController to "PC_MainMenu".

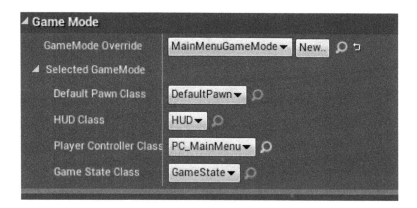

Now that it's been set, we need to configure the Blueprint itself. Double Click the "PC_MainMenu" blueprint in the Content Browser to open it up!

PlayerController = Conduit!

Step #1 - Within the "PC_MainMenu" Blueprint; Create a new Variable ("Int" again!) and call it "PC_Graphics".

Step #2 - In the Main Blueprint view, Right Click (Ctrl + Click) and create an "Event Begin Play" node.

Note: From now on, I believe you should know how to create nodes (Right Click [Ctrl + Click]) to bring up the CBL and search for the node you need. So I will no longer be telling you how to create nodes!

Step #3 - Create a "Does Save Game Exist?" node. This node does exactly what it says on the tin!

In the "SlotName" input, type in "Settings".

What is "SlotName"? When we eventually create a Save Game, this will tell the Blueprint where to look in the Save Game file! When we create the Save Game, we'll tell it to save the information into the "Settings" slot.

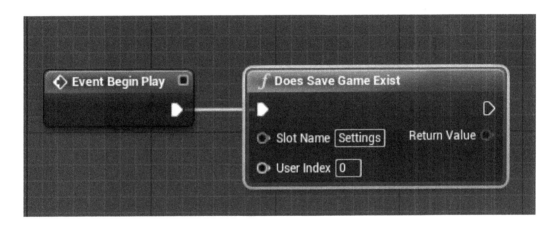

As this node poses the question: "Does Save Game Exist?", We have to give the node the ability to answer the question.

Step #4 - Create a "Branch" node (Which is essentially a "True or False" node) and hook it into the output pin of "Does Save Game Exist" and the "Condition" pin into the "Return Value" pin of "Does Save Game Exist".

We're now going to set what happens if a "Save Game" doesn't exist. Everything we create in the next few steps will stem from the "False" output of our Branch.

SaveGame = False!

If a SaveGame doesn't exist, we're going to have to create it!

Step #1 - From the "False" output of our "Branch", create and connect a "Create Save Game Object" node.

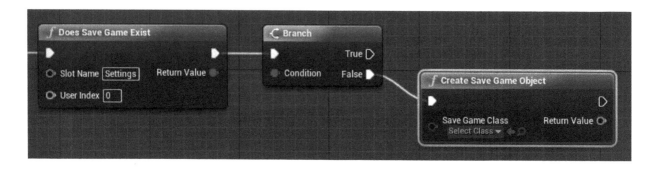

Step #2 - Within the "Create Save Game Object" node, set the "Save Game Class" under "Select Class" to "Save_SaveGraphics".

Now we need to tell the Blueprint that "SaveGraphics" is a thing and give it permission to mess around with it's variables.

Step #3 - Grab the blue pin "Return Value" and drag to the right. Type "Promote" and select "Promote to Variable".

In the Variable Window, Name this newly created Variable to "SaveGame".

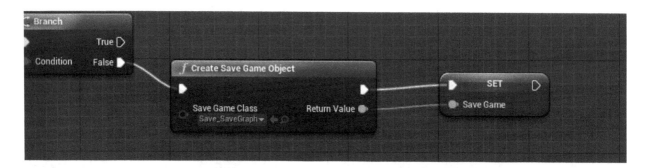

To make sure everything works alright, "Get" SaveGame from the Variable Library, put it into the Blueprint and drag from the output, typing in "Cast" (Select: Cast to Save_SaveGraphics) and connect this after the "Set SaveGame".

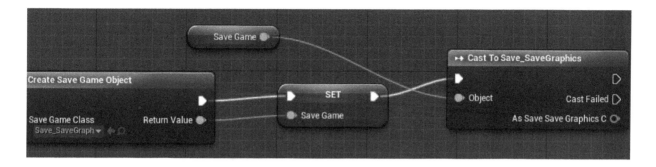

We've now created the Save Game Object, it's time to go back to the "Branch" and branch off to if the "SaveGame" is true!

SaveGame = True!

Instead of Creating a Save Game (As if the Branch is true, it already exists), we now have to "Load" the Save Game.

Step #1 - Create a "Load Game From Slot" node and connect it to the true from our "Branch".

Step #2 - Just like we did before, Set the Slot Name to "Settings" and this time drag the SaveGame variable from Variable Library and "Set" it. Hook the inputs of "Set Settings" to the right output of "Load Game From Slot" and hook the "Return Value" into "Set Settings".

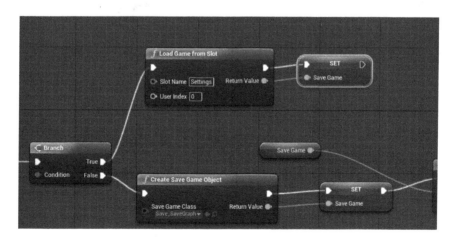

The reason we've done this is because if the Branch was false, we were setting the "SaveGame" variable. However, if the Branch is true, then obviously the Blueprint won't execute any of the "False" code.

Step #3 - Just like what we did in the "False" set of events, "Get" SaveGame and use it to "Cast to Save_SaveSettings".

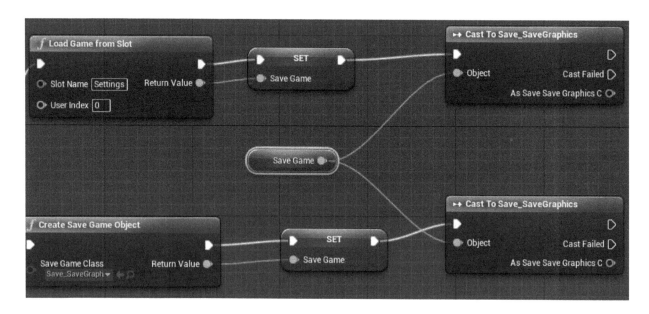

Step #4 - From the "As Save Save Graphics C", click the pin and drag to the right and type in "Get Graphics" and select it.

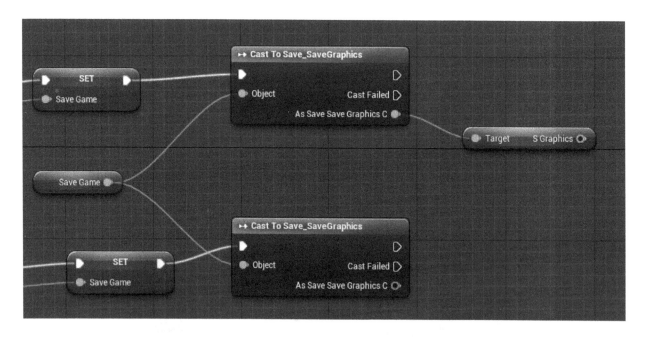

Step #5 - In the "Variable Library", drag in "PC_Graphics" and select "Set". Connect this to "Target - S_Graphics" and the top-right pin of the "Cast to Save_SaveGraphics" node.

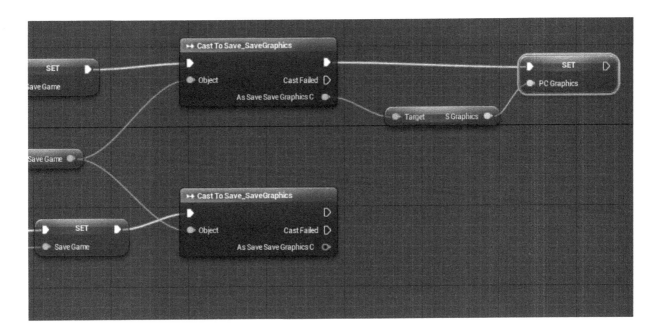

What did we just do? - We're telling the Blueprint that whatever the "Save_SaveGraphics" setting is for "S_Graphics", that is what is what we want "PC_MainMenu"'s "PC_Graphics" to be too!

It may be a tad confusing at the moment, but don't worry - Pretty soon everything will make sense!

What I want you to do now though, is to create the "Switch On Int" and "Execute Console Commands" exactly as they were back in the UMG's "Apply" button. For the Input though, use the "PC_Graphics".

You should end up with something like this:

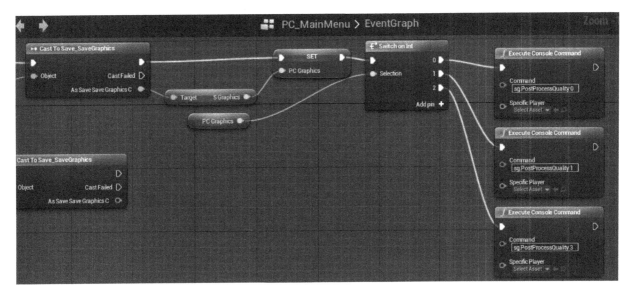

And this is the whole Blueprint for "PC_MainMenu" so far:

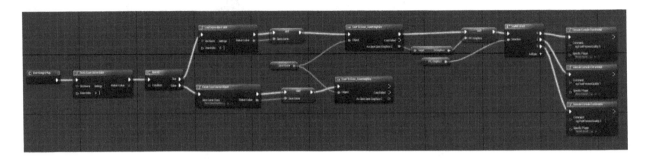

What we need to do now is set it so that when we press the "Apply" button in the UMG, it will save the changes. Here's how we're going to do that.

On Button Press, Save Our Settings!

Step #1 - While still in our "PC_MainMenu", create a new event ("Event Tick"). This means this code will fire every single frame!

Step #2 - In the "Variable Library", create a new Variable. Set it to a Bool and call it "Apply"!

Step #3 - Create a Branch, and connect it to the Tick and bring in the "Apply" bool and attach it to the Branch.

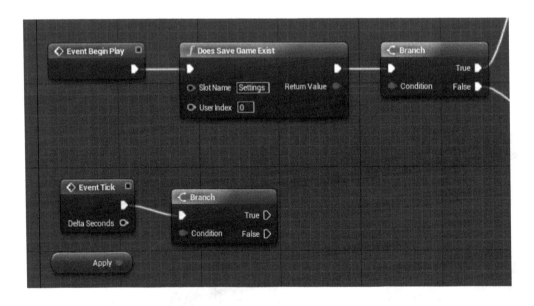

If Apply has been pressed, then we need to alter the "Save Game" file to store the new information.

Step #4 - Grab the "SaveGame" variable from the "Variable Library" and use it once again to cast to "Save_SaveGraphics" and connect this to the "True" of the Branch.

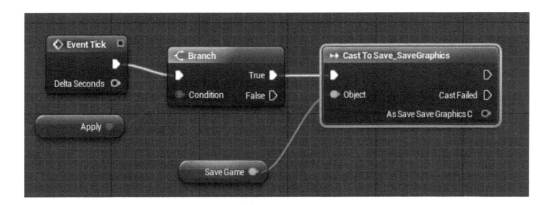

Step #5 - From the "As Save Save Graphics C", click the pin and drag to the right and type in "Set S Graphics" (Not "Get!") and select it.

Step #6 - Bring "PC_Graphics" into the Blueprint via the Variable Library once again and hook this into the "Set S Graphics" node.

Step #7 - From the right-hand side output of "Set S Graphics", create a "Save Game To Slot" node and connect them together.

Step #8 - Grab the "SaveGame" variable from the "Variable Library", drag it into the Blueprint and connect it to the "Save Game Object" and Set the SlotName to "Settings".

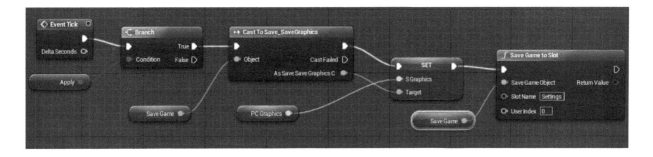

Step #9 - After "Save Game To Slot", grab "Apply" from the "Variable Library" ("Set" it when asked!) and set it to false (By leaving the checkbox unchecked)!

And we're done with this Blueprint! There's only a couple more things left to do; So what are we waiting for? Save & Compile the Blueprint then you're free to close it!

The final few steps will need an adventure back into our "MainMenuOptions" UMG Blueprint!

The Final Showdown!

Once you're back in your "MainMenuOptions", go into your "Graph" view. Open the "EventGraph" which should be in a tab above the Blueprint view. In case it's not, you can find it near the top of the Variable Library.

Step #1 - When in the EventGraph, we need an "Event Begin Play" but they don't work in UMGs. We can however use the UMG equivalent "Construct". So do just that - Create an Event Construct node.

Step #2 - Open the "Compact Blueprint Library" and type in "Get Player Controller".

Step #3 - From the "Return Value" pin of "Get Player Controller", Click and Drag to the right. When the "CBL" opens up, type in "Cast to PC_MainMenu" and connect it to the "Event Construct" node.

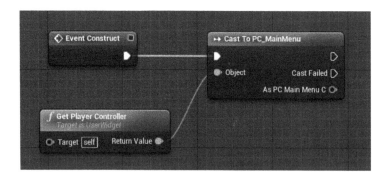

Step #4 - From "As PC Main Menu C", grab the pin and drag to the right. Type in "Get PC Graphics" and select it.

Step #5 - Go into your "Variable Library" and grab "GraphicsSettings" and drag it into the Blueprint and when asked, select "Set".

Step #6 - Connect the "Set GraphicsSettings" to the top empty output pin of the "Cast" and connect the "Get PC Graphics" output into the "Set Graphics Settings" node.

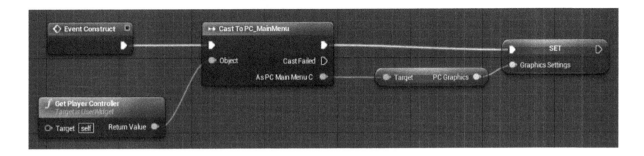

We're now so close to the finish line I can almost taste it! Save & Compile this Blueprint, then go into your "Designer" view.

Click the "Apply" button and where we created Binds before, there's a little magnifying glass next to the name of our "Bind" we created for it before. Click the magnifying glass to open it's Blueprint.

Step #1 - Alt+click the left-hand side input of "Switch On Int" to break the connection to the start of the Blueprint as we need to add a few more nodes here.

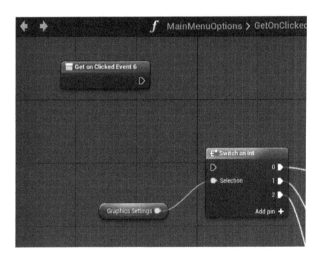

Step #2 - Just like before create the "Get Player Controller" node and use it to "Cast to PC_MainMenu".

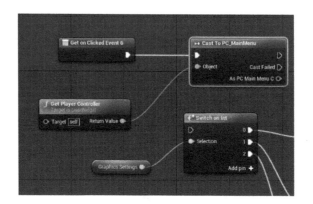

Step #3 - From "As PC Main Menu C", click and drag to the right. When the "CBL" opens up, type in "Set PC Graphics". Once the node has been created, click the pin next to "As PC Main Menu C" once again and this time type in "Set Apply".

Step #4 - In the "Set Apply" node, tick the box inside it to set "Apply" to true and connect this node into the output of "Set PC Graphics".

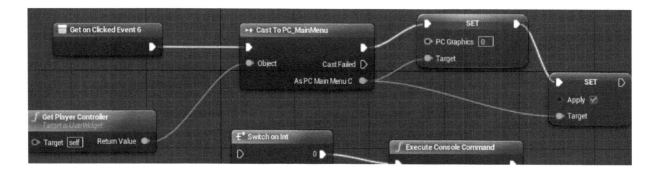

Step #5 - Head into the "Variable Library" and drag "GraphicsSettings" into the Blueprint. When asked, select "Get" and hook this into the "Set PCGraphics" node.

Now simply connect the output on the right of the "Set Apply" node and hook it into the "Switch on Int" node that we created in this Blueprint earlier.

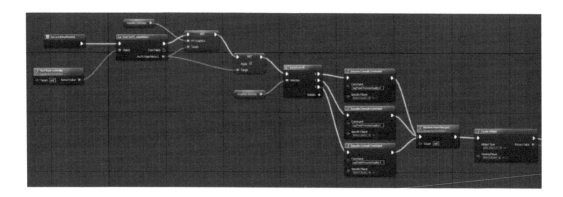

End Of The Book!

Is this the end of the book or the start of Book #3? Who knows!

In all seriousness, this has been an absolute blast! I've loved writing these books and I will continue to do so to help each and every one of you!

As always, if you've got any questions or if you'd like to show me what you've created with this book, then don't delay - email me today! - contact@kitatusstudios.co.uk

I hope you've enjoyed reading and I'll see you next time!

Peace out!
-   Ryan S, Project Lead @ Kitatus Studios.

www.ingramcontent.com/pod-product-compliance
Lightning Source LLC
Chambersburg PA
CBHW060506060326
40689CB00020B/4649